I WiLL Be...

An amusing story of learning to love who you are.

Written by Susan Pivero
Pictures by Jo Renfro

I Will Be...

An Amusing Story of Self-discovery and Learning to Love Who You Are

Published by Berndog Press LLC, Sheridan WY

Copyright © 2022 by Susan Pivero
First Edition

Library of Congress Control Number: 2022907157

ISBN 979-8-9860673-1-5 (hardcover)
ISBN 979-8-9860673-0-8 (paperback)

JUVENILE FICTION / Social Themes / Self-Esteem & Self-Reliance.

Illustrations, layout and cover by Jo Renfro

info@berndogpress.com

To my Gina,

forever inspiring others by being true to yourself.

Always ..." Just be Gina"

Mac feels sure someone will
take him home from the market.
But then...

"Why is that sweet little girl picking a peach?
Don't you want to take me home instead?"

"And why are those people picking all the other fruits?
Hey everyone! What about me?"

Mac feels like a McIntosh failure. He questions his entire apple being.
Until...

...a PEACH!

Mac rolls in wispy dandelions until his nose tickles and he's covered in frizzies and fuzzies. He NUZZLES into a bushel of peaches.

a BLUEBERRY!

Mac takes a
giant breath in

-HHHHH-

and holds it
and holds it until
he turns BLUE.
He rolls dizzily into
a crate of blueberries.

Everyone that picks him up, puts him down. Mac is an unhappy apple being a blueberry.

a STRAWBERRY!

Mac lays in the bright sun. "Ouch! No sunscreen!"

Then he gently places his burning, speckled fruit-self into a basket of strawberries.

Everyone that picks him up, puts him down. Mac is an unhappy apple being a strawberry.

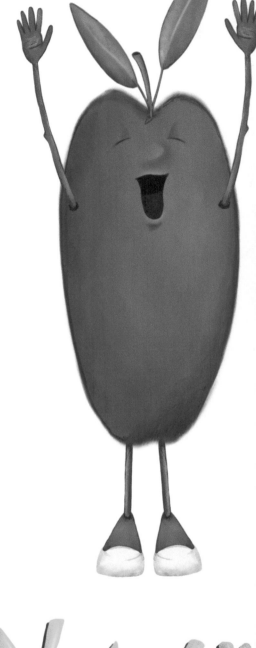

"So maybe not a strawberry.
Maybe I will be...

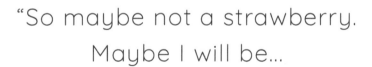

a BANANA!"

Mac **STREEEEETCHES** himself long to the core. He
wiggles like a worm and inches into a bunch of bananas.

Limping from
the banana stretch,

stinging with the
strawberry sunburn,

huffing and puffing
from holding a
blueberry breath,

sneezing from the
peach-fuzzy dandelions,

Mac gives up and heads toward
the pile where the bruised fruits go.

On his way, Mac notices
something interesting in the
market window.
"Wait! Is that... can it really be...
ME?"

"Maybe I don't have peach-fuzzy skin. But mine is smooth and shiny. Hmmm... kinda beautiful"

"And I may not be blueberry blue, or strawberry speckled, but hey! I'm all kinds of pretty reds and I'm adorable. I like my reds!"

"And so what if I'm not banana-long or super tall. Look at me! I have my own fun, curvy shape!"

YES!
I will be...
Just be Mac!
Just be Mac!
Just be you!
Just be Mac!
Just be yourself!
Just be Mac!
ACHES
BLUEBERRIES

Mac snuggles into a bushel with his apple buddies.

And then...

Special Thanks

"I Will Be..." came to be from the overwhelming inspiration of my amazing daughter Gina. I wrote this book because of her, thanks to her, and for her. I have witnessed her manage challenges, accept opportunities, and make smart choices - with a commitment to "Just be Gina" - simple but strong words that she and I have shared through every stage of her life. Gina is Gina! I say that with limitless love and adoration, and hope that in this book I have captured the importance of being yourself, as demonstrated in life by my Gina. Love you forever Sweetie.

Then there's my husband, Bruce, a.k.a. Mr Wonderful. THE MOST patient and supportive partner in existence! He has seen and heard and read and reread my ideas over and over without complaint (at least not out loud!). Thank you Bruce, for demonstrating the theme of this book by teaching and modeling to Gina and me your own mantra: love yourself.

I am blessed with three fill-my-heart-with-love grandchildren. Thank you Derek and Wyatt for previewing my book before anyone else, and giving it your thumbs up. And you my sweet Genevieve . . . your anticipated birth this year was my emotional motivation to see this 20+ year project through to its end. Your new life brings new meaning to mine.

Thank you to my sisters Patti, JoAnne, and Gina (the original Gina in my life!) for your encouragement, and Mom, for your generous gift to start me on my self-publishing way. Thank you to my nephew Chad - your business savvy got me through the most intimidating part of this process.

Professionally, I am in awe of the SCBWI as an invaluable resource, specifically the Northeast group, where "Monday Mingles" launched my decision to move forward and publish. Thank you to the critique groups of peers and colleagues for welcoming me, and your candid yet gentle reviews that helped reshape my story. I am especially grateful to Lisa Cloherty, Eric Sondergeld, and Bruce Shutts - fellow Indie authors - for the time and help you so generously have given me. Thank you Jennifer Rees from Reedsy for bringing my story alive in your editing.

I hold special appreciation for Jo Renfro, whose illustrations give life to this book. Jo, I was hooked on your artistic style and creativity when I first saw your portfolio, and every skinny-legged colorful image you produce continues to make me smile. The incredible imagination you pour into everything you create is wonderfully unique and exceptional. Thank you for accepting my revisions of revisions so graciously. Thank you for sharing your talent with me and every child who gets to know and smile at Mac.

Finally, my thanks to you, the readers, for welcoming us to your bookshelf. And to all and anyone else who offered a positive word on this writing and publishing journey, you know who you are, so BE who you are! Please accept my sincere gratitude.

Susan

CPSIA information can be obtained
at www.ICGtesting.com
Printed in the USA
BVHW020821160822
644712BV00009B/575